ENCOURAGING

A

FRIEND

WITH

OUR

TRIALS

JAMIE PULOS-FRY

ReadersMagnet, LLC

Encouraging A Friend with Our Trials
First Copyright © 2013 by Jamie Pulos–Fry
Copyright © 2023 by Jamie Pulos–Fry

Published in the United States of America
ISBN   Paperback: 979-8-89091-228-2
ISBN   eBook: 979-8-89091-229-9

The opinions expressed by the author are not necessarily those of ReadersMagnet, LLC.

ReadersMagnet, LLC
10620 Treena Street, Suite 230 | San Diego, California, 92131 USA
1.619. 354. 2643 | www.readersmagnet.com

Interior Design by Jamie Pulos–Fry and Dorothy Lee

"Thank you for your testimony of going on for God despite the trials you have suffered. That is such a blessing and challenge to me. I'm sure it will be to others as well."

— **Mrs. Suza Rasmussen,** instructor, West Coast Baptist College, Lancaster, California

"Thank you for your servant's heart and constant joyful spirit. You've been a blessing to me."

— **Miss Jill Kobernat,** instructor, West Coast Baptist College, Lancaster, California

Revelation 21:7 says, "He that overcometh shall inherit all things." Overcomer is a word that exemplifies the life of Jamie Pulos-Fry. Jamie is an overcomer. So many times she could have given up. She could have quit, but instead she pressed on.

Jamie overcame many of life's trials and losses and inherited a peace and joy that can only come from the Lord. Her story will encourage all who read it.

— **Mrs Ginna Dunwoody,** instructor, West Coast Baptist College, Lancaster, California

DEDICATION

This book is dedicated to a special friend whom I wish to keep nameless, my family, and church family.

Thank you to my special friend: I would like to thank my special friend for many things he did to help me with my spiritual walk.

First, by dealing with change and not making it a big monster anymore;

Second, by showing me in the Bible about the reason the Lord tells us not to drink wine. There are many passages in the Bible about this, but the one that convinced me was Proverbs 31: 4 - 8. *"It is not for kings, O Lemuel, it is not for kings to drink wine: nor for princes strong drink: Lest they drink, and forget the law, and pervert the judgment of any of the afflicted. Give strong drink unto him that is ready to perish, and wine unto those that be of heavy hearts.*

Let him drink, and forget his poverty, and remember his misery no more. Open thy mouth for the dumb in the cause of all such as are appointed to destruction."

This verse also gave me the courage to give away all the wine in the house and to tell my family that I do not drink anymore. My family has been honoring me and my beliefs by bringing non-alcoholic drinks to the family get-togethers;

Third, my special friend showed me how it is very important to memorize Bible verses and read your Bible through at least once a year, because you never know when someone is going to ask you a question about it. I still read my Bible every day and really enjoy reading the encouraging messages from the book of Psalms every day.

Thank you, Special Friend, for passing through my life for a short time.

Now, for thanking my family: I would like to thank my Daddy (James John Pulos) for being there during this loss of walking trial. I do not know where I would be today without his help and guidance through this trial and many others.

I will miss you, from your loving daughter (Jamie Joanne Pulos).

In loving memory of my father who passed August 29, 2011.

Husband, Jack Allen Fry, who passed August 5, 1993.

To my church family: Thanking you for listening to my story at the beginning and supporting me when it turned into this book project.

ACKNOWLEDGEMENTS

The book is a result of the efforts of many people, and I am thankful for their generous contributions.

First, I'm thankful to my parents: James and Ellen Pulos, my sister Deborah Pulos, and their lifelong commitment to me. I'm thankful for them being there through my loss of walking trial in my life.

Second, I wish to thank those godly women who have been my examples through the years. Many are still encouraging me through their consistent godliness: Mrs. Sharon Coats, Mrs. Gina Dunwoody, Mrs. Jo Ann Eaton, Mrs. Nancy Lusk, and Mrs. Edie Taylor.

I'm thankful for the love, patience, and encouragement during the season in my life that brought this book to be. Thank you.

Third, I would like to thank those who helped with the proofreading, designing, and publishing of this book. It would not have come to be without all your hard work. Thank you.

Fourth, I would like to thank the Lord for giving me this trial, so I could share it with a kind and giving heart for others in this world. Thank you. Amen.

TABLE OF CONTENTS

FOREWORD

This story came to be a book because of a friend noticing something about another friend of mine.

This friend noticed that this special friend of mine had some strange thing going on with his leg. He called it pigeon-toed. [What? I have known this person for over two years and served with him and did not notice it before.]

So a week or two later, I was standing on the second story of the Revels building. While looking out the window, I noticed him stopping then walking by. Then I noticed that he was not pigeon-toed; it was his knee and it was swollen more than it should be.

"I was wondering if this was the person that I heard had an accident a year ago or two." I was told about it, but the person who told me did not know the person's name. So, I let it go and went on with my life.

So, I tried to talk to my special friend about it. I just wanted to hear his story and give him my encouraging story about my accident. After giving him a note, he took it all the wrong way. It is very hard to lose a friend because of a big misunderstanding.
I will always keep this person in my prayers and wish him a great life and wonderful riches in his future endeavors.

INTRODUCTION

Do trials matter? Yes, our trials have a reason. There are so many questions we ask ourselves during a trial. One of them that most ask is, "Why does God let this happen to us and allow us to go through difficult, trying, painful times in our lives?" We notice that God is all powerful and could stop these trials if He chose to. Yet, most of the time He does not.

Therefore, there must be some reason for them, some godly reason for not sparing us these hardships.

Once we begin to understand God's reason in our lives for these things, we will be able to stand strong through any storm of life.

The reason I chose to write out one of my trials in life was to encourage someone that did not know they needed help in their own trial of pain at the time. They were not willing to listen at the time, so I started my short story for others.

From some teaching at my church and research in my Bible, I have learned that once we understand the source, with knowledge and wisdom, it gives us the reason and purpose for the trials. Wisdom helps us to question the heart of God by asking, "Lord, why have you allowed this? What would you have me learn from this?"

Some people think asking God for help is wrong and are uncomfortable with the idea of asking God "Why?" God is our Heavenly Father and just like our earthly father, He wishes us to ask questions. The fact is, we need to ask Him why certain trials happen, because we want to extract as much good from our suffering as we can.

- **First, God gives us trials in order to test our faith.**

This can be shown in many verses in the Bible like 1 Peter 1: 7 (King James Bible: Cambridge Ed.) "That the trial of your faith, being much more precious than gold that perished, though it be tried with fire, might be found unto praise and honour and glory at the appearing of Jesus Christ."

"The purpose of these troubles is to test your faith as fire tests how genuine gold is. Your faith is more precious than gold, and by passing the test, it gives praise, glory, and honour to God. "(God's Word Translation [1995]).

God is trying us to give us faith, so we can prove His strength:

- **Second, God gives us trials in order to test our devotion to Jesus Christ.** True devotion demands that we follow Jesus faithfully, no matter what we are going through. We still need to obey Jesus even when we do not understand what is going on.

- **Third, God gives us trials in order to cleanse our lives.** Trials have a way of pushing things to the surface – bring hidden sins, bad habits out. We must look at them to become that mature Christian who God wants us to be.

- **Fourth, our trials give God that time to show us His sustaining power for His people during tough times.** Now is when you can show your great testimony to unbelievers who may see you going through a very difficult situation while still maintaining the peace of the Holy Spirit.

- **Fifth, a main reason for God giving us our trials is to have a Christ-like character within us.** Our trials show us that we cannot live apart from God. Having a Christian life is not about being good, but Jesus Christ living with and through each and every one of us. We need to surrender to His will, so we can react better to stress, trials, and suffering so He lives out through our lives.

- **Finally, trials give us equipment through God to serve others.**

2 Corinthian 1:4 shows us this very clearly.

But, 1 Corinthian 10:13 (ESV), says "No temptation has overtaken you that is not common to man. God is faithful, and he will not let you be tempted beyond your ability, but with the temptation he will also provide the way of escape, that you may be able to endure it." So, God does this to make us more useful in helping others.

So when we fully understand and see that someone else is going through pain, we will be able to reach out to them where someone else may not be able to. This is just knowing first-hand what the person is going through. If we have been through the same issue ourselves, then we can have understanding of what that hurting person is going through and what they may need at the time of their trial.

CHAPTER ONE

Life At This Time

MARRIAGE STATEMENT

TO HAVE AND TO HOLD, FROM THIS DAY FORWARD, FOR BETTER OR FOR WORSE, FOR RICHER OR FOR POORER, IN SICKNESS AND IN HEALTH, I PROMISE TO LOVE AND CHERISH YOU.

I was married to Jack Fry for nine months when we found out he was very sick. We had been dating for many years by this time. We thought he was putting weight on because he sat a lot on his job. Then he fell and hurt himself at work and they took him to the hospital. We found out that his lungs were not working and they needed to put him on the waiting list for a lung. He was living on an oxygen tank.

Lung transplants were experimental at this time. They told us in the interview that they would try to find the closest size replacement and blood type. Plus, the doctors told us that the steroids would take away most of the food nourishment and he would have to take a lot of pills. Because he was in his early 20's, his immune system was very strong and there's always a chance for rejection of the new lung.

The lung transplant was only to prolong your life, to do that last special thing in your life. The doctors also told us that if the heart goes, they will not revive you.

My husband played D & D back then and wrote a game for the Dungeons and Dragons Tournament. He flew to New York six months after being put on the lung transplant list. He was happy to have the game judged and he came home knowing that he finished something he started in his life. [This was the hardest thing for me to do, to let my husband go with an oxygen tank all by himself on a plane.]

My husband became a lung transplant recipient because of a work-related accident. While he was working for Lockheed as a security guard, he was asked to work with that black bird that was flying around and we did not know what it was. It was called the Stealth Bomber. It was experimental at the time.

The fuel for the plane was experimental and the guards were opening the gate and pushing the plane out to test it. The fuel was making all the security guards sick all in different ways. Things like feet issues, hands, cancer, brain tumors – they were all dying of something or very sick.

There was a lawsuit for it. But the fuel went into and out of my husband's body and did its damage and left no trace. They even did a spinal tap to see if they could find something. But they could not. So we were not able to collect anything for the case.

He was in the hospital for lung rejection when I got into the accident. Plus, we were both young at the time and my husband did not think about changing his life insurance papers at work. He did not change the beneficiary on the policy to my name. So when I went to claim them, his mother was the beneficiary on his life insurance policy. I cannot change what life gives me. Sometimes life does not always work out the way you plan. I hope she used it in good health.

CHAPTER TWO

Car Accident

PSALM 20:1-5

May the LORD answer you in the day of
trouble;
May the name of the God of Jacob defend
you;
May He send you help from the sanctuary,
And strengthen you out of the Zion;
May He remember all your offerings,
And accept your burnt sacrifice.
May He grant you according to your
heart's desire.
And fulfill all your purpose.
We will rejoice in your salvation,
And in the name of our God
we will set up our banners!
May the LORD fulfill all your
petitions.

This is a true story that happened over twenty years ago. On November 2, 1992, I was coming home from visiting my husband at Cedars-Sinai Medical Center in Beverly Hills. He was a lung transplant recipient at this time.

I was coming up to Ave S and the 14 freeway when my car started vibrating. This was the park-n-ride area from Palmdale. The freeway at this point is going on an upgrade. Plus, in front of me, the freeway would be going through a craved-out mountain on the left side. The right side was coming to a high upgrade off ramp with a fence, dirt road, and small grass pasture down below.

I noticed that there was a car coming down the slow lane around the overpass, and I thought I had enough time to get over. Everything felt like slow motion at this time. The last thing I remember seeing was the mountain and stars, and then I hit my head.

I do not remember seeing the car that hit me. I went flying off the freeway and rolled around three or four times down the hill and hit the fence. (I wonder now where would I be today if that fence had not been there?.) I remember waking up at the Palmdale Community Hospital hallway on a gurney. I was still fading in and out and heard the nurses talking about moving me to Lancaster Community Hospital. Then I faded out again.

CHAPTER THREE

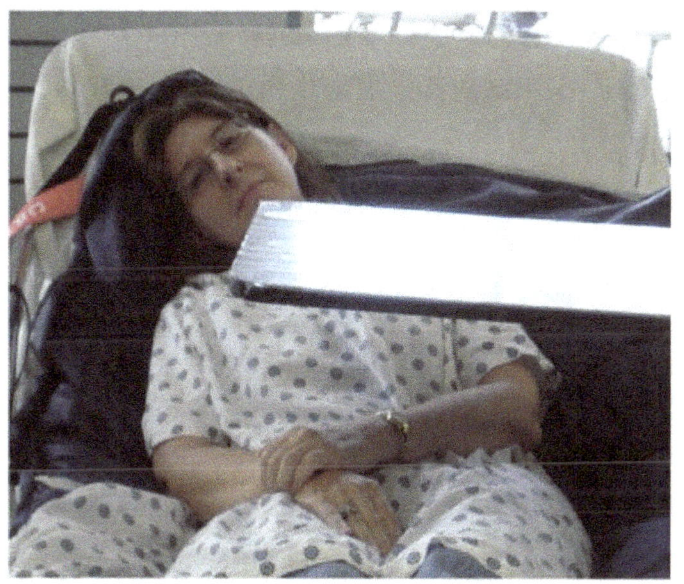

Hospital Room

PSALM 28:7

The LORD is my strength and my shield;
My heart trusted in Him, and I am
helped;
Therefore, my heart greatly rejoices.
And with my song I will praise Him.

I woke up to find out that I had an arm harness and was in a hospital bed at Lancaster Community Hospital. Because of the cracked collarbone, the hospital kept me for three days. This helped me to learn how to eat with one hand. The nurse showed me how to put on the arm harness so my collarbone can heal properly. I was talking to the nurse and noticed my father was standing by the door of my hospital room. I was wondering why he was standing there and not by my bed.

The nurse asked me to get up and walk to the door and back to my bed. I said, "My leg does not move." She said, "That is okay; you have not broken anything. You have bruised every muscle in your leg from the hip down to your toe."

I got up and walked to the door and got back, dragging my lifeless leg. Imagine a small hospital room and only having to take a total of 10 steps to get to that door. It took me about 10 minutes to get there and back. They ordered me a walker to take home.

Then they asked me to walk down the hallway with my father helping me. The hospital had ballet handles on the walls of the hospital hallways. Dad had to help me on the way down because of my left arm harness. On the way back to the room, I was able to help myself with my right hand. They sent me home. Then I looked in the mirror and found out that I had glass in my face and arm under the skin.

I do not remember if I had any visitors, but my mother remembers me coming home with some flowers.

CHAPTER FOUR

Parents

MATTHEW 9:22

But Jesus turned around, and
when He saw her, He said,
"Be of good cheer, daughter;
your faith has made you well."
And the woman was made well
from that hour.

I did not go home to Lancaster, California. There was no one there to take care of me. I could not drive or walk at this time. I got home to Van Nuys, California, where my parents still live. I could get into bed, but they had to lift my foot and put a pillow under my blankets so I could sleep at night. [It is very hard to go back to your parents' home to be taken care of as it is, but it was especially hard this way.]

This went on for around three months or more. My father had been taking me to the insurance attorney office to go over my case; they kept asking me to repeat what happened over and over again. They were trying to get me to remember if I hit the car or the car hit me. I blacked out when I hit my head on the windshield and still do not remember until today who hit whom. I had to talk to my attorney at least three times and to their attorneys two times.

This was when I found out from the police report that I was hanging from my seatbelt when the emergency vehicles found me at the fence and not at the street.

I had to talk to their attorneys. I ended up being found guilty of the accident.

Fortunately, the insurance company paid for everything. I think about it now and realize this really helped me let go of the anger, bitterness, pain, and fear of the accident.

If you have been in an accident, please talk to someone about it. It is never a good idea to harbor pain. It not only affects your life and others around you, but also your spiritual walk with the Lord. It stops your growth in so many ways. Yes, we all know that we need to give it to the Lord to help heal the pain. What most of us do not know is that the only way the Lord can help is by bringing people into our lives. These people can help take away the bitterness that we do not know we are still holding inside us.

CHAPTER FIVE

Peanut Butter and Jelly Sandwich

PSALM 31:1-3,24

In You, O Lord, I put my trust;
Let me never be ashamed;
Deliver me in Your righteousness.
Bow down Your ear to me,
Deliver me speedily;
Be my rock of refuge,
A fortress of defense to save me.
For You are my rock and my fortress;
Therefore, for Your name's sake,
Lead me and guide me.

One day, my father left me alone in the house. I was sleeping and he thought he had time to get something done and I would be fine all by myself for a few hours. Well, I woke up and was very hungry. My bedroom is on one side of the house, and the kitchen is on the other side of the house.

So I got up from bed and lifted myself up to the dresser. I reached out to the bookcase with

stuffed animals on top of it, dragging the dead leg behind me. I got to the end of the bookcase and reached for the bedroom door handle, pulling my body to the door frame. Next, I reached out to the living room door frame, and pulled myself out into the hallway bathroom door frame. Then I pulled myself to my father's accordion desk in the dining room.

I got to the dining room and I had a dilemma... should I take the china cabinet or the dining room table next to tackle? I chose the dining room table and pulled myself to the end of the long table and worked my way over to the china cabinet. I got to the end of the china cabinet which put me in a hard place.

The next thing I needed to get to was the piano which was ten feet away. So I chose to reach up and hold onto the hallway door frame above me to pull myself to the piano. (This is a hallway that leads to my parents' bathroom and bedroom.)

I was almost to the kitchen, pulling my body to the half wall and beam that divides the dining room and the kitchen. I got to the kitchen table and pulled myself up tall to reach out to the cabinet that holds the bread box, silverware, and peanut butter. I still needed to pull my body over to the refrigerator around the corner for the jelly (strawberry, not grape). I made my strawberry peanut butter jelly sandwich. That sandwich tasted like prime rib with mash potatoes, gravy, and strawberry shortcake all in one. So yummy!!!

Guess how long that sandwich took me to make? It took me two hours getting there and back to my room. What I am trying to say is that I did not give up. Have that kind of focus for everything you do in your life.

The Lord gave me a purpose that day and every day in the future. I was put on this earth for a reason and that was to help other people around me. That is why when my Bible teacher gave me a spiritual gift test to take a few years ago, I noticed that I was very high in every case, but the highest was being an encourager.

CHAPTER SIX

God's Image

ISAIAH 41:10,13-14

Fear thou not; for I {am} with thee: be not
dismayed;
for I {am} thy God: I will strengthen thee;
yea,
I will help thee;
yea, I will uphold thee with the right
hand of my righteousness.
For I, the LORD your God, will hold your
right hand.
Saying to you, 'Fear not, I will help you.'
"Fear not, you worm Jacob, You men
of Israel! I will help you," says the
LORD and your Redeemer, the Holy
One of Israel.

We all make mistakes in our life, but please remember we have a wonderful God out there to help us. He helps us by bringing people into our lives to share their trials and to encourage us. When going to the doctor to remove the glass fragments around my right eyebrow and forehead, there was not a request to remove the glass in my right arm. I still have it in my arm after 20 years because when I asked the doctor to do it for me, he forgot to do it, and I never pushed the subject. It is only on the top surface of the skin and looks blue-green in color. If you ever see me in a short shelved blouse or dress, you might notice it.

I still have a piece of glass in my arm from that accident to remind me of why I am here.

The Lord could have taken my life that day, but He gave me a second chance. We have to remember that we are made in God's image and He does not make mistakes or errors. We are the ones that damage our bodies with the bad choices we make. He could have said that it is your time now and I do not need you anymore. Please remember there is a reason why we are all here and that is to bring people to the Lord and serve Him until it is our time to go from this earth. The Lord is the only one who knows that time and place.

CHAPTER SEVEN

Special People

PSALM 38:4-6, 9;15-18;21-22

For my iniquities have gone over my head;
Like a heavy burden, they are too heavy for me.
My wounds are foul and festering because of my
foolishness.
I am troubled.
I am bowed down greatly;
I go mourning all the day long.
Lord, all my desire is before You;
And my sighing is hidden from You.
For in You O LORD, I hope;
You will hear, O Lord my God.
For I said, "Hear me lest they rejoice over me,
Lest, when my foot slips, they exalt themselves
against me."
For I am ready to fall,
And my sorrow is continually before me.
For I will declare my iniquity;
I will be in anguish over my sin.
Do not forsake me.
O LORD, O my God, be not far from me!
Make haste to help me,
O Lord, my salvation!

There are people out there who are disfigured and have problems with walking and talking. These people could have been born with them or had an accident to have these issues. The Lord looks at them as special people and we should, too. They have to work a little harder than most people do. These people are joyful in doing things for the Lord.

There is one lady I work with who has taught me to slow down and really listen to others when they are talking to me.

Also there is one Gentleman I work with who has taught me to have patience and not to be in a hurry when going from place to place and to enjoy the world around us.

I remember one early spring day, walking from one school building to another, where a butterfly was just hovering there right in front of me. I just wanted to reach out and touch it. But instead, I just watched it dance in front of me for a few minutes. It was amazing to see the gift that the Lord created that day.

They do not ask why anymore. They do things just to give people a smile as a reason not to give up. I enjoy working and being part of these people's lives every day.

CHAPTER EIGHT

Serving in Pain

ISAIAH 40:29

He gives power to the weak,
And to those who have no might
He increases strength.

Now remember on that day of the accident, I was hanging from my seat belt. Let's fast forward ourselves to 18 years into the future - to the present time. Recently, I am taking classes at West Coast Baptist College as a church member auditing classes. I woke up one morning in severe pain. I was crying the whole time I got dressed on the bathroom seat. I thought it was because my bedroom mattress was old and the couch pillows were worn out. I got them replaced and did some stretching every night before I go to bed. It helped some. I did this for six months. It hurt to stand or walk on cement. My foot was asleep while I was singing in the choir every week. I was also volunteering in the Great Awakening Coffee Shop and Book Store; I served the college students at lunch and dinner once a week. This was like having a second Sunday to serve the Lord. I did not say anything to anyone, because I saw that a lot of people at church served in pain just like I did.

CHAPTER NINE

Being a Blessing to Others

COLOSSIANS 1:10-12

That ye might walk worthy of the Lord
unto all pleasing,
Being fruitful in every good work, and
increasing in the knowledge of God;
Strengthened will all might, according to
his glorious power.
unto all patience and long suffering with
joyfulness;
Giving thanks unto the Father, which
hath
made us meet to be partakers of the
inheritance of the saints in light.

I had left for a training event in Dallas, Texas, which lasted a whole week with a lot of standing and sitting. I came back with no break in between and served in the music ministry at my church. Because of the pain from my back, I almost fell forward while singing in choir. If it were not for that friend who was standing by me, and holding me back with their arm, I could have hurt myself and many others around me.

I decided to find a doctor that week. (I have been going to Frye's Chiropractic for a year and a half now.) They told me that I had sciatica and two pinched nerves in my lower back, and that they could see from my x-ray that it was from an accident I had over fifteen years ago.

It has been a year and half now and I feel almost normal. During that time, I lost a sister, an aunt, and a father and still kept serving the Lord with a joyful heart with all the people around me who served the same as I do.

CONCLUSION

As we have seen, our trials can be of value to others. With that in mind, let's take a look at a few ways that an understanding of God's reasons for trials might lead us to the right response.

- *First, within the first chapter, "Life at This Time,"* we learn that we do many things for our loved ones. We must understand that God is in control of the timing and strength of our trials.

- *Second, within Chapter Two, "Car Accident,"* I wondered where I would be today if that fence had not been there. So we must realize that God has a reason for each trial in our life.

- *Third, within Chapter Three and Four,* we see it is very hard to go back home and be taken care of by our family as it is, but it was especially hard this way. We must see that each trial is given to us to meet a specific need that God sees in our lives. That is, that we need help even if we don't want it at the time.

- *Fourth, within Chapter Six "God's Image,"* like it shows us by reading Isaiah 41, "Fear not, I will help you." So we must accept that each trial is going to result in our own goodwill, if we do it in faith. God will always be there. We just need to ask for help.

- ***Fifth, within Chapter Five "Peanut Butter and Jelly Sandwich,"*** we see when someone should not focus on their trial but take a look at their trial's usefulness in measuring their spiritual walk.

  For example, because we have been through this trial ourselves, we are more useful in handling a powerful hardship that could have crippled us a few years ago. This is because our continuing trials have taught us that God's will indeed empowers us to keep going.

- ***Sixth, within Chapter Nine "Being a Blessing to Others,"*** we see that when we think we have been through a trial, the Lord is always teaching us more. We must be sure that God will be there with us, through every step of the way.

- ***Seventh, within Chapter Seven "Special People,"*** we see there are people who are disfigured and have problems. But with faith and by God's grace and enabling power of the Holy Spirit, we will not only survive, but we will also go through and over each trial.

- ***Eighth, within Chapter Eight "Serving in Pain,"*** here, the Lord is teaching us that our trials can come back to hurt us and we may not even know why. We must be happy and joyous in that each trial has a reason for God to show His power to sustain us under tremendous pressure. We must search how each one of our trials can strengthen our faith by proving that we can depend on the Lord for all our needs.

When we are a child of God, we can see that the Lord has us on this earth for a reason and mine is to be a blessing to others by serving and encouraging others around me even if they do not want the help. There are times that I do not feel up to encouraging others, but with the Lord's help, I can do it with a smile and keep going. So please keep smiling. Be in your place. Do it for that person who may need you someday.

"Our Trials Can Turn Into A Blessing With God's Helping Hand"

Making Choices

Thank you Lord for choosing me,

Guiding me to make the right choices.

Thank you, Lord, for choosing me to be a blessing to others.

Having this relationship with you, a loving heart to share with others.

Help me to make the choices with your guiding hand.

Glory to God for all the people He chooses to walk with me every day.

Glory to God for the love He chose to share with me today.

Praise to you, Lord for choosing me, giving me the wisdom to serve you every day.

Help me to make the choices with your guiding hand.

Praise to you, Lord, for bringing peace into my life with your guiding hand.

INDEX OF SCRIPTURES

About the Author

Jamie Pulos-Fry is a member of Lancaster Baptist Church in Lancaster California. She has a servant's heart by serving in music ministry, volunteering in many parts of the church and for the West Coast Baptist College. This is her first book and hopes this blesses and encourages others with her story.